THE 3 PILLARS FEEDING THE HOMELESS

AUTHOR & FOUNDER MEMBER:
MICK PESCOD FOUNDED 2016

JOINT FOUNDER MEMBER & TRUSTEE: GED DEMPSEY

Hi Mick

Thanks for this. I think it so important that there is a permanent record of what has happened over the years. Well done!!

During my tenure as PGM there were various significant things that happened of which I am very proud. Sheaf Close is clearly my lasting contribution to the Province. I am also very pleased with the New and Young Masons Club which I feel is so vital in securing the future of our organisation. But looking back, I feel perhaps the most significant thing was 3 Pillars. I did very little apart from encouraging you and Ged and made the important statement that 'you must not fail'. Mick, you certainly have not failed and the operation continues to expand. It does, of course, place Freemasonry in a very good light, but the principal effect is that many needy people are receiving assistance. We said at the beginning that it was to provide 'a hand up' and not just 'a hand out' and there are some amazing stories of how you have assisted people back into society.

Mick, I will forever be grateful for what you have done. It is so amazing.

Best wishes

Max

Past Provincial Grand Master Max Bayes

PREFACE

As we all quickly found out, working on the front line at Peterborough, feeding the homeless was a roller coaster of emotions.

Sadness, horror, laughter, anxiety, all mixed in.

There were never 2 evenings the same.

Each evening when we were leaving the feeding station, we all felt a great relief that we had a home to go back to.

Some of the people we served had some truly terrifying experiences.

We thought our charity would blend in perfectly with freemasons in the community, being there on the ground working together with other like-minded people.

Eight years on, we think it has been a success.

Read the book and make your own mind up and we would love any feedback.

In the book you will read and see some graphic & true stories of some of the lives and incidents of these people.

A chance encounter, the seed was sown…..

Six years ago, we had a family weekend in London.

We saw a show and stayed in a lovely hotel,
On the Saturday morning we caught the tube to Oxford Street and went shopping.
The family branched off in different directions and I did my own thing.
It was a very cold and wet morning and I walked passed a shop doorway, there were 3 very bedraggled men sitting on some makeshift blankets, looking the worse for wear and freezing.

I felt so guilty, watching all the shoppers walking by, I turned round and asked them if they wanted a hot meal and drink.
They looked at me suspiciously, but there was a McDonald's just up the road, so that's what I offered them, and they accepted my offer.
It took about half hour, but I returned with 3 party packs including big mac, fries, a sweet and piping hot coffee. They were so very grateful.
I carried on feeling quite pleased with myself, but started thinking, what will they do for food tomorrow.

Returning home, I was still thinking about the 3 guys,
I picked up my freemasons magazine, and lo and behold, there was an article about homeless in Peterborough, about a group called the forget me not trust.
It was actually 2 freemasons feeding the homeless, looking for volunteers.

I enquired straight away, and joined them.

Hope you enjoy reading this book

as much as I have enjoyed writing it

Thank you for your support

Mick

They were two brothers who had a building firm, and they supplied hot dogs, chocolate biscuits and coffee, which looked like gravy, from their van.

The problem was, their business obviously came first and they couldn't guarantee turning up regularly. They basically left me to get on with it.
Not having suitable vehicle, I borrowed my son in law, Andy's van, "Thanks Andy!"
Stocked up with food, a couple of tables from my garage, and I was up and running.

My first visit, I only had a handful of visitors, but it built up rapidly.
Karen Gibbs, who helps run caring for Cambridgeshire homeless, heard about me and agreed to drop some food and sleeping bags to me, where I was feeding the homeless at the brewery tap car park.

When she turned up, I had a queue of over 20 homeless and struggling.
My prayers were answered as she stayed and helped me give out the food and drink, and saved the day.

Shortly after, W.B.Ged Dempsey, who had also heard what I was doing, joined forces with me.

The two main problems:

    a. We urgently needed a van.
    b. We needed storage space, as I was using my garage.

My son, Darren offered us free use of his business premises The Mortgage Broker Ltd, we used his old double decker bus for storing all of our goods.

(Darren & Lita Pescod)

On the Saturday I bought a big van and at hockey with Darren, we were watching his daughter playing hockey, he sent out a few messages to his friends to help sponsor it. Within 15 minutes, he had received pledges for almost £2000!!
This really helped me towards the costs involved.

That same year, Andy Walker who was worshipful master of Euston lodge, also gave us a significant donation from his charity list.

The van was named the "Green Pig" by Vernon Paine. It was green, sturdy and ugly and I must say very reliable.

We were now really in business!

We started asking for volunteers from the general public and the freemasons.
Over the first couple of years we built up a strong team of volunteers. About 85% of our volunteers were members of the public, mainly women and the rest freemasons.

(Ali Pearce & Toni Bourne – 2 of our original Magical Fairies)   (John Lumley who has been supplying food since we started)

We even had a resident cat called "Ginger" who kept the bus rodent free & was always there with a friendly welcome for the volunteers.

Thanks to Ged who was giving talks at various lodges, we started receiving donations from lodges and individuals. We also received donations from many organizations in the St Neots area. For example, T.D Autos, courtesy of Rebecca & Tony Dixon, look after our St Neots van. All repairs, mot, all free of charge.

(Left to Right: Myself, Rebecca Dixon- T.D Autos, Darren Pescod, Vernon Paine, Kevin Hull-Premier Plus & Tony Dixon- T.D Autos)

St Neots Golf Club gave us a large donation from the Captains charity that paid for the St Neots van. The brand new purpose built van that replaced the green pig, was a donation from an anonymous Peterborough freemason & my son Darren sorted many donations from local business colleagues.

After about 2 years, we became an official Freemason's charity and our provincial grand master, Max Bayes assisted on the front line. He didn't know what to expect, but soon got stuck in serving the food.

(Our provincial Grand Master, Max Bayes)

One day, I had a message for help come through, his name was Brian, and he needed food, sleeping bag, shower facilities, in fact he had very little.
He was sleeping in the back yard of Boots chemist & we took some clothes, provisions etc.

My wife Lorain & I arranged to meet him, outside Sainsbury's in Huntingdon.

Brian's story:
He ran his own internet business.
His wife had a terminal illness and died
The business went bankrupt
His house was repossessed
He went into a deep depression
His family disowned him

There he was homeless with absolutely no support…and that's how quickly life can change!

We had a meal at Sainsbury's & Brian told me the thing he missed most of all, apart from his deceased wife, were mature cheddar cheese and branston pickle sandwiches I spoke to Karen Gibbs, who helped run a Cambridge charity & through a local business, she arranged shower facilities, use of the shop's microwave & kitchen for Brian's personal use.

Ged contacted YMCA who own some flats in Peterborough, and he was provided with accommodation.
As a thank you he started running our I.T, as this was neither Ged's nor my strong points.
As he had managed to get back on his feet, and resume a sort of normal life again, He applied for and was accepted for a position at Perkins engines.
After a year, he moved out from YMCA into his own privately rented property.

He has regained his dignity. He is now housed (thanks to the YMCA), working and off the drink and has regained his self-respect.

Recently (6 weeks ago) he called W Bro Ged on a Sunday apologised for bothering him to tell him that he had been promoted to Head of IT and would be soon able to vacate his room in the YMCA for another deserving person since he will now be able to rent his own place. He has a company car and a significant salary

He thanked the W Bro Ged and asked him to thank W Bro Mick for giving him his self -respect back, his life and providing the bridge for him to rejoin humanity.

The best reward the charity could ever receive & we wish Brian well.

Eventually we had around 60 volunteers.

A rota for the front line, collectors of food and donation's, volunteers for emptying, cleaning and restocking the van and storage facilities.

Vernon named these helpers, "the magic fairies". The name came about when one of our drivers, said, he had returned the van in an awful condition, but when he went to pick up again, it was fully stocked and clean. He couldn't believe it.

At this time one of members of our Euston lodge at Eaton Socon, W.B, Steve Barrett, manager of the priory centre and his two cooks in the canteen, offered to heat up our food. The jacket potatoes were supplied by John Darlow free of charge, which we serve with baked beans and hot dogs.

Before lockdown we were giving out over 100 hot dogs, 120 halves of 60 large potatoes, 12 tins of baked beans & cheese per visit.
We also were giving out donations from Tesco's, Aldi's and Greggs.

No food went to waste as all surplus food was taken up to Knott's farm to help feed the animals.

8 volunteers per visit, on the front line serving food, hot drinks, clothing, sleeping bags, tents & toiletries. On every visit, driving into the Brewery Tap pub car park, there was a mighty adrenalin rush, one never knew what to expect.

Some examples:
There might be 10 visitors waiting for us or there might be 80 there.

There was an enormous amount of pushing and jostling, so one of our key volunteers and drivers, Vernon Paine organised a system.

Volunteers stood van side of the trestle tables, there was an organised queuing system, and if there was any arguing, they were sent to the back of the queue.
All hot food, sandwiches, hot and cold drinks were given out first although we kept some back for latecomers.
Then all the cakes, donuts etc & when that was finished, we would open up the back of the van. This was where we supplied all the clothes, sleeping bags, tents toiletries etc.

The homeless would sit around kerbside in small social groups, enjoying their food and drink. It was normally a happy occasion. But there were exceptions.

Here are some of my earliest experiences, both shocking & humorous that arose:

A woman in her late thirties, I guess, turned up at the Green Pig & she told me her story. She had a large bust up with her partner and grown up family, walked out of the family home. She couldn't find any accommodation and so lived in a derelict car. The previous night, someone had smashed the window whilst she was in there and had stolen what few possessions she had.

She was still in shock when she turned up and was too humiliated & embarrassed to return home. Our ladies, as always, sorted her out with all her needs and we paid for a night in a hotel, so she could get her senses together.

We never heard from her again.

One nasty bit of work actually pushed one of our lady volunteers quite heavily; this resulted in the guy getting banned. He was always after extra food clothes and not a pleasant character.

We had an Eastern European group who would pinch whatever clothing they could get their hands on working as a team. They were subsequently banned.

There was also a National Front issue & one night, this got a bit nasty.
On our next visit they were sitting near our pitch in a group.
I knew the ring leader from recent visits and went over to the group.
I addressed him, telling him that they must promise not to cause any problems otherwise we would turn the van around and drive away and not serve anyone.
This had the desired effect. Thank goodness!

One polish lady turned up with burns and bites on her face and was in a terrible state. Her tent had been set alight with her still in it, and then she was attacked.
She had a part time job and needed clothes etc., so that she could still go to work.

She was taken into back of the Green Pig, and two of our lady volunteers gave her a complete change of clothes, toiletries, cosmetics, sleeping bag & new tent.
She was a new woman when she emerged from van.

While all our volunteers were kept busy, I used to walk round our visitors to see if anyone needed anything else and check if they were okay.

One bitterly cold and wet night, a young woman was in floods of tears, she only had a summer dress on & had just been evicted from her flat , no possessions, nothing.
I took her back to the Green Pig and our wonderful volunteers again gave her a complete change of clothes, cosmetics, toiletries and one of our visitors who she knew offered her temporary accommodation.

A lady turned up one evening, unannounced and set up a table next to us, giving out glass bottles of soft drink.

Our rules prohibited any glass and Vernon, who was the driver, and therefore in charge of operations that night, went over and told her she couldn't continue.
She went ballistic, saying 6 policemen had savagely beaten her up and raped her.
Vernon replied that he knew nothing about that but that she couldn't set her pitch up there. She demanded Vernon's name and he wouldn't give it. She started asking all our other volunteers, what was his name & someone piped up "Mick".

Well thanks very much Sheila Wren, I still have not forgotten that.😎😎

Daiva, a young attractive Eastern European lady was homeless, due to the fact that she had a lovely little dog and wouldn't part with her dog to secure accommodation. She had a part time job and used to sofa surf where she could. One evening, just as we were closing up for the night, Daiva always used to help us clear up. A late comer showed up but all the food had gone so Daiva opened her rucksack and gave him her supplies which she was going to have after work. Eventually Daiva, along with Rui and Emma became regular volunteers for us.

One evening when I was walking around and chatting, on my return to the van, I couldn't get through as one of our regulars was sitting on the plastic box, at the side of the tables, blocking the entrance. He was absolutely out of it, I asked him several times to move but he then knocked the coffee urn off the table, picked up the plastic box, to hit me over the head with it.

Within a milli second, a little Polish girl in the queue, rushed up, jumped on his back and had both her hands round his neck. About 10 others then jumped him and dragged him away. He made a very swift exit. He didn't reappear for a couple of months, and when he did appear, he kept a very low profile,

I would never have ever thought it was remotely possible. A large English lady started turning up every visit and she was very loud and always was at the front of the queue whether it be for food, clothes or toiletries.

To be honest, I was getting fed up with her, when there was a row going on between her and a couple of our lady volunteers at the toiletry counter. She had half a dozen boxes of tampons in her hand. I told her, she could only have one (box).

With which she pulled a tampon out of the box and waived it above her head shouting what the f—-ing use is one tampon to me. Everyone was in hysterics & she ended up with one box.

Some months later she reappeared.

She donated us some clothes for the homeless. Apologised for her past behaviour, due to serious depression and the medication she was on, informing me, that she had been given her old nursing job back.

A very pleasing outcome!

There used to be an elderly Sri Lankan man, Stan, visit us regularly.

He lived in a very small housing association studio apartment. He was diabetic, so there were only certain things he could eat, so we used to prepare a separate pack of food for him. He was a very quiet gracious man. One evening he asked to have a chat with me.

Informing me he had won a prize in a newspaper competition. The prize was a top quality sports bike & he wanted to donate it to the 3 Pillars.

We offered to Ebay the bike on his behalf and give him the money.

He wasn't having that, so we drove round to his flat and picked up the bike. I believe from memory that the bike fetched £400 donated to the 3 Pillars and he wouldn't accept a penny. It was a thank you from him for all the kindness the 3 Pillars had shown him.

Victor was a small young man in stature but had a very large mouth on him.

He was always trying to help us and loved shouting orders at his fellow homeless. His partner on the other hand was a very large lady. He didn't turn up to their tent one night and the next day at our feeding station……..she was waiting for him.

She gave him a real dressing down in front of everyone and then gave him an almighty slap on his cheek, which turned crimson. The homeless and all the volunteers howled with laughter as Victor walked off, tail between his legs.

Another incident, when I was the object of ridicule.

I had assigned all the duties on one evening, leaving myself to serve the pot noodles, which had been donated to us. I set about the task with relish, pouring the contents into an empty plastic cup and then adding hot water.

One of our visitors was amazed and asked what I was doing. She burst out laughing and soon everyone joined in, homeless and volunteers together. Well in my defence, I had never had a pot noodle, that's my story and I am sticking to it.

After about one year, we had an Indian family turn up with hot food and they joined us serving all their exquisite treats. They were with us for over a year but unfortunately, had to stop due to ill health of two of them. No, it was nothing to do with their cooking.

One evening, Rui turned up.

A Portuguese man, down on his luck, who was okay until he had a drink. Then he wouldn't stop talking.

His wife had thrown him out of the family home and he was homeless. My son, Darren allowed him to sleep on the bus, which was kept at his business car park in Eaton Socon for the night.

I gave him sausage and chips and Darren took him some toast for breakfast. Pip, my adopted daughter, picked him up & took him to Peterborough to attend a court hearing regarding visitation rights to see his children, neither of whom were aware he was sleeping rough. That's what you call good service.

He loved to help us when he could and had the low down on all the homeless, whether or not to give a sleeping bag out to different individuals. He was a source of information.

He was a chef by trade and we managed to fix him up with a job with accommodation. He is remarrying and has invited Ged and myself to the wedding.

(Left to Right: Rui with Chris & Dave, two of our regular street friends & helpers)

One night a fight broke out and the guy that was on the wrong end of it evidently phoned the police, without our knowledge. Five minutes later, 3 police cars sped up to us in car park. Out of one of the cars jumped Katie Piper, with a microphone doing a documentary for Channel 4, asking us about the incident. The lady police inspector, in charge of the team, also asked us questions about the incident.
As they left the scene, she turned round to our team and said, "Keep up the good work", which was a real tribute to our volunteers.

Andy was a very quiet, subdued Romanian lad. He would always hang about at the back of the queue, fearful of crowds. One evening when was I walking round chatting to various people, I had a chat with Andy.
He had a tent in the nearby woods and was building a log cabin type arrangement, between the trees. He was very proud of it and would show me pictures of it on his phone, with the various stages of his work.
He was terrified it would be seen by others and damaged. He became more confident, talking to all the volunteers & always staying behind, helping us to clean up rubbish left in the Car Park. We always carried 3 empty plastic dustbins in the van and strategically placed them around the Car Park.
We saw Andy picking up scraps of food and placing them in his bag. We asked him why and he replied that they were for a mouse who he found wandering around near his tent; it regularly came to visit him.
I can tell you, that story bought a few tears to our lady volunteer's eyes, myself and Ged's included.

The most horrific things we have seen were in two entirely different occasions, men were discharged from different hospitals in the early hours of the morning, both had very serious injuries and they eventually got directed to us for help.

The first man, who turned up with his partner, had suffered serious stab wounds to the chest. They were sleeping rough in a shop doorway on the East coast, the lady was attacked by unknown assailants, and he tried to fight them off and was stabbed.
He was airlifted to a hospital in our region and the surgeons managed to save his life. He lifted up his shirt and showed us these horrendous stab wounds on his chest.

The second case, the man involved spoke very little English and arrived with a woman who was trying to look after him. He was in his tent, late at night, when assailants unknown, set fire to his tent. Dousing it with paraffin, or something similar, while he was asleep. Again he was rushed to hospital, he suffered very serious burns all over but he survived and again found his way, courtesy of the lady, to our feeding station.

In both cases, neither of the victims has anything but the clothes they were wearing. Our wonderful volunteers fed them, clothed them and made them comfortable.

One of the best things about our charity, apart from our volunteers, is that we can make instant on the spot decisions. We took both these individuals to nearby hotels and paid for Bed & Breakfast, for a couple of nights, contacted the Council, who arranged accommodation for them.

They were regular visitors to our Feeding Station for a few weeks before drifting away, to where? We don't know.

We do appreciate that we couldn't do these things without the marvellous support we receive from Freemasons, Lodges, Businesses and the General Public, of which we have over 5500 Facebook members.

I know we shouldn't have favourites but I had a couple.
Jas and partner Andy.
Jas had many problems, very very thin, drug addiction but when alert she was bubbly, lively and wouldn't stop talking.
Seen in the photo with myself, she always gave me a hug.

Andy, on the other hand was a big man, quiet, very friendly, all round nice guy.
He would defend Jas with his life.
We looked after them as best we could & they used to sofa surf when they weren't on the street.
I brought Jas a small colourful bracelet back from my annual winter holiday. She was absolutely over the moon, and treasures it. I received a call from Andy, he had been offered a caravan to rent.
The 3 Pillars supplied him with furniture and white goods. This was fine for about 6 months until his benefit money was changed and he couldn't pay the rent for a couple of weeks. He found out the true character of the owner, when he was told to leave the caravan immediately, otherwise he would have all his fingers cut off!
This is how it can be when you are only just getting by.
There were two teenage twins that used to visit us on a regular basis, both homeless, both very muscular and their father was also homeless. The girls were quite violent at

times especially when drinking. Most of the homeless including their father, kept out of their way on these occasions.

One evening, a foreign lady turned up, she had severe mental health issues and was throwing stones at everyone. For whatever reason, she attacked the twins with a can of drink, which she had turned into a jagged weapon. It was a fierce encounter until some of the homeless managed to stop it, with the twins getting the better of the encounter.

When the twins were sober they were fine, but if drunk, they were a problem and we had to quieten them down. They were not very popular; however on one particularly dark and very cold evening, we pulled out of the car park to drive home. Huddled together on the pavement against the wall of the Brewery Tap pub, were the 2 girls with blankets and sleeping bags that we had provided, trying to keep warm.

One of our volunteers WB Kevin Reynolds, from St Ivo lodge, said he had never been so cold serving the food, in all his life. We all had lovely warm homes to go to and we were leaving the girls behind and all the other homeless fighting for survival.

All of the 3 Pillars team, especially those on the front line, who could see how desperate some of the people were, were affected and it was so very important to us all to know, at least we had given them a little respite from the awful situation they had found themselves in, most of them through no fault of their own.

Christmas day, lots of places were offering food for the homeless, the Churches and other organisations, so we decided to have a Xmas meal with presents on Boxing Day afternoon. Someone printed out leaflets in all different languages, regarding what was happening and times and these leaflets were passed around the week before.

Justine Hughes assisted by Charlene Engelbrach for the first year and assisted by Moira Brown for the second year, organised all the presents and asked for donations, sorted them all out and wrapped them all up. There were almost 200 Xmas boxes, consisting of gloves, woolly hat, warm socks, underwear, chocolate, crackers and other items.

On top of that Karen Keech, who runs the Caring for Cambridgeshire homeless group, was doing a similar thing but gifts were wrapped up in large pairs of woolly socks. She had over a 100 presents left over. She gave these to us, so we were giving out presents throughout January as well.

I am always away over Xmas, so it was left in the capable hands of Ged & Vernon and then Lee & April Garner.

It's a massive operation to sort out food. Karen Walker, wife of Andy from our Euston lodge, is landlady of the Barley Mow pub and provided the turkey for all 3 years. Sarah and mum, Jerry, made a fantastic soup come stew, which was very popular. Sarah incidentally has been extremely ill in hospital these last few weeks but we received a message from her brother very recently, saying she seemed to have turned the corner. Our thoughts are with you Sarah.

Tracy & John Darlow, cooked the Potatoes, Pip & my granddaughter, Scarlet, the jam tarts as well as cakes and so many others of our organisation chipped in. One of the homeless guys provided the music and some wonderful Boxing days were had by one and all.

On the leaflets handed out, there were instructions to hand back the leaflet to receive a present. One guy had collected 6 and asked if he could have 6 presents.
I heard a whisper that there was some Champagne going round but that remains unverified

Case Studies from Ged Dempsey, Trustee

How we have helped:
'You can't change the world, but you can change somebody's world'

Set out below are just a few examples of how the 3 Pillars-Feeding the Homeless has helped individuals;

Case Study 1: Sean a 62-year-old male came to the feeding station December 2017 (remember the snow that year) he had been discharged from hospital at **04.30** that morning. He was wearing beach shoes, no socks, chino pants and a collarless T- Shirt. His whole body was shaking with the cold and his teeth were chattering.

We gave him a coffee which he spilt down his front because he was shaking so much, and he started to cry. The whole team was upset. We placed him in the van and dressed him in thermals and warm clothes and there was a suggestion to give him a tent and a sleeping bag, but it was agreed that if we did this it was likely he would be dead in the morning. The decision was made to book him into a Travelodge which we did for 4 nights and then the YMCA was able to allocate him a room.

Sean was a graphic designer he was responsible for the artwork that sits on breakfast tables of two popular cereals. Following a marital breakdown and the demon drink he lost his way, his house and his dignity. He is now housed (thanks to the YMCA), working and off the drink and has regained his self-respect.

Case Study 2: Stephen a 59-year-old male, major issue with alcohol and had been homeless for 13 years. He was too ashamed to tell his family he had been made homeless so just 'disappeared'. It took several months for him to engage with the team but eventually he expressed a request for help. He wanted to change his situation and get help with the alcohol issue that had taken him down.

We did eventually get him help and were able to get him housed in the YMCA and he promised he would contact his family to let them know he was ok. We did get a call some weeks later, 'Hi, I have contacted my two daughters on Tuesday and went to see them both. They have both been married since I last seen them, and I met my 3 grandchildren for the first time. Did you get on ok, 'yes I just spent all day crying'

Stephen is in contact with his family and his Grandchildren and is now working in a major supermarket stacking shelves, off benefits and off the drink.

Case Study 3: We had a phone call from a Police Sargent (who had seen our Facebook page) at 18.30 they had been called to a cricket pavilion following the siting of a person acting suspiciously. Arriving they found a 42-year-old man dishevelled, freezing cold and in pain. He was a veteran who served in the two Iraq wars and was discharged following a major injury which resulted in half the back of his left leg being blown off. He was suffering from PTSD and his partner had thrown him out because she could cope with his mood swings.

The Police Sargent (who was also ex service) took John back to his home and persuaded his wife to take him back in but only on the basis that he would sleep on the floor in the front room.

The Police Sargent called W Bro Ged to explain that there were 3 children in the house, no food, no electricity or gas, little or no furniture, children sleeping on camp beds and Mum on the floor with blankets. The benefit had been stopped because he was late for an appointment at the DWP.

The family were visited that night by W Bro Ged, food was purchased and £50.00 each put on the gas and electric cards. Two days later Bro Matt Horton and Bro Dan Cooke delivered Beds, 3 Piece Sofa, coffee tables and wardrobes along with many other furniture items. The 3 Pillars- Feeding the Homeless provided a kettle, toaster, iron and microwave together with sets of plates, cutlery and other household items.

We shopped for a further two weeks for the family and W Bro Albert Bareham then fitted the house out with carpet. John is now having medical treatment for his PTSD and so far, all is well.

Case Study 4: When at Court on a Friday morning W Bro Ged received a call from one of the Independent Domestic Violence Advisors (IDVA). They had an emergency, a victim of Domestic Violence (DV) who had been advised that her ex-partner was being released from jail the following Friday and she was in meltdown. She had 3 children and had been subjected to a violent and serious assault, fracturing her skull, and 2 broken bones in her leg following a stamp.

They needed to move her from Cambridgeshire to Canterbury in Kent, but it needed to be done on Monday and nobody could know where she or the children were.

A call was made to a Brother (W Bro Paul Henry – Wardle & Keech) who owns a removal company and the situation was explained to him and without hesitation the answer was yes. This was done on the Monday free of charge and we trust that the family are now settled in their new home.

What did surprise us was the number of females that are on the street who are vulnerable and at high risk since the streets are volatile at the best of times taken to the Housing Office who provided temporary accommodation.

****

 At this time Ged was busy trying to arrange help and accommodation for the homeless and he was very successful. To date, the 3 Pillars have arranged through the Council, the YMCA and Housing Associations, over 116 homeless people into accommodation and over 60 into employment.

We started feeding the homeless and vulnerable people in St Neots, it was a far lower key than in Peterborough and we used to see about 15 people on average. Considering that most of our volunteers and a lot of our donations came from the people, businesses and associations in the St Neots area, it seemed the right decision to look after our local people who needed help.
We again provided hot food, drinks, clothing, toiletries and any other items that were requested. It was all very much appreciated by all of our visitors.

Royal Recognition

On Thursday 16th July 2020 The 3 Pillars-Feeding the Homeless were invited to attend the Garden House in Peterborough where we were presented to HRH Prince William and had the opportunity to explain the work we do in the Community – he was very appreciative of the work that we do and thanked the Charity

Supported Housing Fellowship

BUCKFEST

About 4 years ago, we were invited to a meeting with the Buckfest Committee, to see if our Charity was suitable to become one of their Charity partners.

Buckfest have an event each year at the grounds of Buckden Recreation ground. Capacity for the event is 2400 people and it is sold out every year on day one of ticket issue. The chairman is Rick Holden, who is lead singer of the Junkyard Preachers, a top local group and the other leading lights of the committee are Nicky Warnock & Simon John.

There are over 20 acts, mainly, groups & singers, many food stalls and plenty of children's entertainment. It's a fantastic day out!!

All profits go to local charities and we were asked to take part, because of the type of charity we are, local, well known by the public and willing to pitch in.

We decided to have an annual 3 Pillars Raffle and a tombola. We were asked to sell Buckfest Programmes with all the money going to various charities. The day was a fantastic success!

We were invited to be Lifetime Charity partners and have been going every year since. This year we had 12 volunteers present plus young Zeo, son of Ali and Don Pearce. This is our most important fund raising event of the year.

(Vernon & Steph Paine)   (Myself & a Grand raffle prize)

One of their longest serving volunteers, who is a very elderly, colourful character, had fallen on hard times, and the Buckfest Committee asked us if we could help him.

He lived on an old boat in the marina and it was in need of repair, no heating or lighting, and was quite a distance away so because of this he used to sleep on a bench in the village.

At first he refused all help being a very proud man but we found out that the one thing he really wanted was accommodation in the Village.

Armed with all the facts, Ged Dempsey, went to the Housing Office and it took a time but eventually bingo! he was given a place.

We had donations come in from Buckfest & our supporters, and eventually had all the items required to make the place he was given, his forever home.

A great result all round.

Other large local fund raising events were:

Another Annual event is The Railway Garden, held at Little Paxton, in the back garden of two of our long serving volunteers, Sue and Ivan Page.

Ivan and his son marshalled all the trains, Sue and friends, Ann & Don Murgatroyd, served the food with other help from friends. They really make the event quite spectacular. No admission fee & they hold a raffle. You can sit down and watch all the different types of model trains in action, stopping at stations.

It's a mini Gt. Yarmouth Model Village. All the home made cakes are donated, with ice creams, hot and cold drinks served. All the visitors are made to feel at home.

Final Result: a lovely afternoon with £555 raised for The 3 Pillars Charity.

St Neots Golf Club Captains Charity.

The Captain, Robin Horsler, asked us to be his main charity for the year.

He had heard good reports regarding our charity and his wife Emma Jane also knew us very well. We were delighted and entered two teams of 4 into his Captains Day Charity event.

We didn't do very well, but we were there. Mind you this was only part of the money raised. There were auctions, ladies day raffles and all sorts of other events.

The donation enabled us to buy another van & the "St Neots Van" was on the road.

We owe an enormous thank you to Robin and Emma Jane, the committee and all the players, gents and ladies all.

The RAFA Club St. Neots (The Royal Air Force Association)

Mike Milne, the Chairman, asked us to go to a presentation evening. Mike is father of Fiona Milne, who had volunteered for us. She also helped prepare the hot food for our feeding the homeless evenings, with Caroline from the Priory Centre.
We were presented with a large cheque, and are indebted to all the members for choosing us as one of their Charities.

(Left to Right: Helen Beaumont, Steph Paine, Sue Hook, Lorain Pescod & Kerry Walsh)

Mary D,Cruz, also raises money for us. She runs, on her own, several events, craft fair days and various functions throughout St Neots.
Mary is not a youngster, but has boundless enthusiasm and plenty of energy, and is dedicated to helping worthy charities. Thank you Mary!

****

When we had Lockdown due to Covid 19, our feeding stations had to cease.

The homeless were all put into hotels on a room only basis, funded by the Government. We supplied a lot of the food into these hotels in Peterborough, for the homeless.

 Things started easing up, although it was still a long time before we could start providing food as we were used to, because of the numbers of people grouped together. Government guidelines stated it was groups of 6 maximum.

However one Saturday, I received a message from Greggs Bakers. St Neots
Their freezers and fridges were all broken down, all the food was going to waste, could I help? My answer was yes!

So I drove our charity van down to the shop & loaded up all the fresh food. They promised me, that in future, all left over food at close of business each day, we could have. This was the start of our relationship with Greggs.

Knowing the area well, where all our senior citizens and needy people lived, myself, Darren and Vernon proceeded to bag up all the food & cold called on these people offering them a free bag of fresh food and asked if they would like a regular bag on a weekly basis. It took a few hours but we emptied the van.
Most of the people we saw, were very happy with this arrangement.

Nigel Ingle volunteered to organise these Greggs collections from the St. Neots store as well as the new Greggs store, recently opened in Eaton Socon.
He had a team of collectors, who daily, collecting the food & stored it in our fridges at our base at The Mortgage Broker Ltd.

(Left to right: Lita Pescod, Emma Fletcher, Vicki Hill)

(Lois Bowey)   (Left to Right: Meena Sharma, Lita Pescod & Tyla Pescod)

Shortly after, we started receiving regular donations from Tesco Express, Aldis and the huge Hotel Chocolat Warehouse, courtesy of Tanya Thulborn, all based in Eaton Socon.

We have just received a very large donation of cash from Hotel Chocolat, courtesy of Tanya Thulborn and Yvette. Thank you so much everyone at Hotel Chocolat, for making this possible.

We sorted out volunteers to collect from these stores.

The next job was to organise the volunteers to prepare and deliver the food packs. We had teams of 4 from Monday to Thursday on a rota system, with two people delivering each day. Again this started off low key, but we now give out about 180 bags weekly, 52 weeks a year, and those who need a grocery pack, we supply as well. Deliveries also go to 3 strategic places in Peterborough, where many of the homeless go to benefit from shower facilities & help with benefits paperwork, CVs and job applications.

(Left photo: Vicki Hill receiving a Thank you gift from one of her super senior ladies on her round)

(Right photo: Volunteers Mike Kirby & Rod Bissett

On Friday's our ladies Kerry & Helen who have been with us almost from the start, 8 years ago, along with Marina & Jenny, sort all the clothes, bedding, toiletries and groceries and then we are ready for the new week.

Our rounds have got bigger and bigger due to word of mouth.

One of the familiar faces around St Neots, was a homeless man, Stuart and his lovely Staffy dog, Bailey. Stuart lived in a tent in the riverside park and had a small boat. He was told to move on by the local Authorities and asked for help. We took our van and moved him to another place in St Neots but he preferred to sleep in a tent.

He was always polite and he & his dog were very popular in town. Never actually begging, but if anyone asked him what he needed, if anything, he would tell them. His new pitch was near the river and we used to deliver a food bag to him there. Bailey was also pleased to see us, as were a flock of swans that used to gather close by.
Another young homeless man pitched next to Stuart, they got on well and we also delivered him a fresh food bag.
We also arranged shower facilities at the nearby Priory Centre, thanks to the manageress Lisa.
The one thing they both needed was to be able to launder their clothes. One of our volunteers Bex Johnson, was happy to do this, so twice weekly we picked up the clothes, took to Bex and then returned them when they were ready.
Sadly, Stuart was taken ill last year, we sent a get well card from all our members and it was delivered to him in hospital with many best wishes and messages.
It was one of his proudest moments and he posted it on our Facebook page, for everyone to see.

Stuart sadly died a little later, but his dog Bailey has been given a lovely home by 2 of our Facebook friends.

One of the benefits of currently having over 5500 members on our Facebook page, is they keep us in touch with the needy in our Community.
If there is an emergency of any kind, we are generally the first to hear about it, especially at weekends when there is very little other support available from other sources.

I had a message one Saturday evening from Steves Taxis.
A guy had turned up in their waiting room, absolutely soaked to the skin, he only had on the clothes he was wearing and was the worse for drink.
He had lost all his possessions including his phone and had travelled in on the train. He remembered nothing else. An ambulance was called prior to my arrival, but the paramedic, who examined him, found nothing physically wrong with him and left, hence the call to me.

So, accompanied by Lorraine Hines, who was one of our volunteers and worked for Steve's taxis, I went back to our unit to get him a change of clothes. I could have given him a tent and sleeping bag, but it was a terrific stormy night and I couldn't leave him there. We took him to the nearest hotel, paid for the weekend plus breakfast & Lorraine checked on him Sunday morning.

We picked him up Monday morning and drove him down the housing office, where he was eventually found some temporary accommodation.
It turns out, the guys father, was a very known and popular figure in St Neots, who had died a few years earlier. They had been very close and it seems this was the start of all the problems, both mentally and alcoholism.

There appears to have been an increase in abusive and violent relationship, against women in particular. During Lockdown two cases spring to mind. No names or locations for obvious reasons.

Both had partners, one in prison, who have location restrictions placed upon them. Just before Xmas, we had a call from one young woman with two small children asking for help. She had relocated and as is the norm these days, was given a nice little place with no furnishings whatsoever.

We put out an appeal on our Facebook and were inundated with offers of white goods, furniture, carpets throughout house, which included fitting, food & children's toys. My friend, Ron, donated a double mattress and assisted by myself and WB Lee Garner, we delivered them.

The big van was stacked up with goods & the mother was reduced to tears when she saw all the donations. The last item off was a tricycle for the little boy, his little eyes lit up and he was so excited.
Ron sent me a message that evening saying "the look on that little lads face when he saw his bike, I will never forget, it made the whole day so worthwhile".
The carpets were fitted the following week, and the white goods were installed by her brother.

The second case was similar, a young mum with two small children, nice little place but nothing else. Again we put out an appeal and so many things were donated.
We also took the mum to our unit and gave her a hamper of food to set her on her way.

There were two completely separate emergencies, both concerning the Marina in St Neots.

The first was an SOS from the Church, when everywhere was flooded. A man was marooned on his boat, he was rescued and we gave him clothes food etc and he was given temporary accommodation, until he could return to his boat.
The second emergency, was when a young lady with a baby, contacted us. She lived in a house in St Neots and had an elderly relative who had a run-down boat on the

river. It was unused at that time. Her husband had a history of depression and that was getting worse, he was talking about suicide.

The woman was panicking, she felt she had to get away from the house for the safety of her child and wanted to go the boat, thus she contacted us.

Whilst her husband was away from the house, myself and Jo Whittaker immediately arranged to meet her. We picked up some of her belongings & Jo bought her some toiletries and we also provided her with a microwave.

She stayed on the boat, until the authorities sorted everything out, at least she and her youngster were out of potential harm's way. All this was completed in less than 3 hours.

PEOPLE CAN BE SO VERY GENEROUS:

There was a man, in a poor state, that came to our notice through our Facebook.
It was late at night and he was miles away from his home town having had a domestic row and was forced to leave the family home.

It was another awful night, rain was pouring down and we paid for a night's accommodation in a Travelodge. The young girl at reception sorted everything out and as I was leaving, she called me over and gave me £20 for our charity. How generous was that, probably over 2 hours work to cover that.

Another time, we went to call in our local Aldi's store for their regular donation and there was nothing for us. I told the young girl assistant not to worry as sometimes these things happen. She asked me to hold on for a couple of minutes & she came back with 10 cans of soup and paid for them at the checkout herself out of her own money. Again, what a lovely thing to do!

In the same store on another occasion, I was collecting 150 plus bananas & 30 multibags of crisps, when I received the usual quips from a lady customer, "Was I feeding the monkeys?" I explained about our charity feeding the homeless.
She was waiting for me outside the store & handed me £20.

We had another call from the Church.
A teenager was going to have to sleep rough for the first time in his life.
It was a freezing Sunday evening and he was being given a housing association property the next day. The lad was absolutely terrified, so we paid for a night's hotel accommodation.

Was it a waste of money? Myself and Ged certainly didn't think so.

We can make instant decisions and it means we can sleep well at night, knowing we have helped someone in distress for the cost of a hotel room for the night and I am absolutely certain the ladies who had given us money so generously, would have been so thankful where there donations went.
One of our volunteers, Sheila Wren, contacted us about one of our young men, in his mid twenties, who we give a fresh food bag & clothes toiletries etc to.
We generally try to look after him as he is permanently wheelchair bound.

He lives almost 3 miles from the shops, his mother had Covid and was in a poor way & she usually did all of his shopping.

His one wish in life was for a mobility scooter.

We posted a message on our Facebook page and lo and behold, one of our supporters came up trumps, WB John Rivett & wife Caroline.
Myself and Ged took the Charity Van over to Wellingborough to collect the mobility scooter, we picked up Br. Lee Garner and delivered the mobility scooter on a Saturday morning.
To say the lads face was emotional was a complete understatement. He kept repeating "I can't believe it, I can't believe it, am I dreaming, is this true?" Myself and Ged were in tears, even big Lee's eyes were moist.

(Lee Garner & Ged Dempsey delivering the mobility scooter)

None of us will ever forget that Saturday morning!

We had a call for help from Lois, a young lady who had to be relocated due to abusive relationship.
She had a room in a HMO, (Housing Association Multi occupancy property), to which we deliver to 7 of these properties in the area, with normally 6-7 people in the house sharing a kitchen.
She asked to go on our fresh food bag list & once she settled in, she was cooking for all the other residents. She set up her own car valeting service, but had to stop due to cleaning them outside the property where she was staying.
She decided to go mobile, I had an unused bike, which I gave her, she bought a hoover & a trolley to fit on back of her bike. With the hose & cleaning equipment, she was now up and running.
She cleaned our charity vans, has volunteered to help when we were short on our fresh food bag rounds & a keen volunteer for us at Buckfest.

We wish you well Lois!

Message from Lois: "Thank you Mick, that's so kind, I just want to say thank you for believing in me and seeing what most people don't.
I would not have come this far if it wasn't for people like yourself and the 3 Pillars xx

One of our homeless guy's, was put into temporary accommodation. Eventually he was offered his own flat by the Housing Association & our past Mayor of St Neots, Barry Chapman, had some furniture for him.
We contacted Stephen Ferguson, then our current Town Mayor, who volunteered for us occasionally, to assist, which he agreed, accompanied by our own Bro Lee Garner. In the photo, the 3 of them are flexing their muscles unloading the van and delivering to the door.

(Left to right: Former St. Neots Mayors Stephen Ferguson & Barry Chapman with Lee Garner)

Thank you so much gents, you did us proud.
I was behind the camera; very dodgy knee….that's my story.

(Myself & Barry Chapman Former Mayor of St. Neots Presenting the cheque to the 3 Pillars)

Kerry Walsh, who has been one of our longest serving volunteers, also works in the food bank.

One of her customers was really struggling with a very large hernia just below his stomach, and he had difficulty walking. We went to meet him, and he was living in a closed down restaurant for the past 2 years. The owner knew he was there and was okay that he was staying there, as it showed someone was using the place.

It was 5 miles outside St Neots, in an isolated spot, they had cut the bus service out and he could only afford a taxi to come into St Neots, once monthly on a £25 round trip. He was only on a single persons benefit.

Although out of the way, we started taking fresh food, groceries and clothes on a regular basis. He was also very lonely only coming into town once monthly.

We hope he can soon be operated on and make himself more comfortable, but with waiting lists at hospital as long as they are, unfortunately it could be a long wait.

Update: We are pleased to say that he has just had a successful operation & is recovering well!

I would like to mention a new service that we have in place for those homeless people or victims of abuse, currently living in temporary accommodation, and have been offered their first for ever home.

Our two lady volunteers Cheryl Bryson & Jo Whittaker, regularly take our large charity van, collect donated furniture and other goods, store it all in a unit at St Neots Storage and then deliver, when required, to those that are moving in.

St Neots Storage, kindly give us this facility free of charge and also allowed us to store goods for our Help the Refugees in Ukraine appeal.

Regarding the Help the Refugees in Ukraine appeal, we have currently sent 6 laden vans full of goods, in our large charity van to their central collection Warehouse at Pymoor, Ely.

A big thank you to everyone who contributed & helped with the Ukraine Appeal, especially the committee & members of St. Neots Conservative Club.

We have now also extended our "feeding the homeless" services to Rushden & Northampton.
Emily Jane is now assisting Ged Dempsey in feeding the homeless in Peterborough along with other duties.

Ged Dempsey's report

Rushden:

Rushden started in July 2022 and was delayed due to Covid 19.

We opened at Park Road in Rushden and we serve food there every Wednesday evening supplying all that is needed. It's not a massive operation on average 12-15 people. We deliver the food and clothes to Park Road, and this is managed by W Bro Simon Harker ably assisted by Emily and myself.

Northampton:

This is now our flagship site.

Northampton started on 10th January 2023 at St James Church where we have the full use of the kitchen and the Church Hall. We feed on a Tuesday and Friday at 6pm. On the first night we had no visitors, on the Friday we had 1 and on the following Tuesday we had 3.

W Bro Aaron Day who manages the Northampton setup (who is a member of the local church and conducts ceremonies there) was unsure whether it would be a success, but numbers gradually increased.

The numbers attending each meal is now averaging 60 visitors.

The kitchen has been granted a 5* rating by the Environmental Health Agency and provides a choice of hot meals and desserts.

It supports homeless people, but we have found that in the local community, those that are struggling, including many single parents and children, lonely elderly people and a good mix of ethnic diverse families attend and feel comfortable.

It became obvious that we not only provide food, clothes, tents, sleeping bags and toiletries but we provide a social and safe place for people to meet and talk. Many of our early visitors had made friends with others and request to be sat with their newfound friends.

In addition to providing the food, we also have a 'Foodbank' at the Centre, and they can pick up to 5 items that they can take away with them and we also provide a food take away option so that some members of their families can eat at home.

The team is mainly Freemasons and their partners, but we also have a good mix of non-masonic volunteers. We have great team in the kitchen that come in early to prepare the food and cook it so at 6pm when the doors open we can serve the food this is supported by table service by an amazing team of volunteers.

Two of our volunteers are qualified nurses and they have been indispensable supporting and directing many of our Street Friends to register with local GP practices and even dressing wounds for one individual who had fallen and cut his head and his arm.

In all we provide an outstanding and vital support to this community of which we are immensely proud of.

This operation has been supported in an active sense by our Provincial Grand Master Rt W Bro Mark Constance and his wife Dawn and the Executive with special mention to W Bro Michael Caseman-Jones and his wife Gail who are now permanent volunteers.

This initial project has received valuable support and advice from our previous Provincial Grand Master Rt W Bro Max Bayes who set out the guidelines and principals of operations for the Charity at its inception:

1. **"If you brand this Freemasonry in the community and it fails that is not good for Freemasonry in general or my Province in particular."**
2. **"Once you start this you have to be able to continue it because you will create a dependency."**
3. **"Most importantly you cannot just be a hand-out you have to be a hand up, so you have to find a way to break the cycle."**

The above set the principals of operation for the Charity and we have since August 2016 housed 188 people via support agencies that we work with, and 84 Street Friends are now in work, off benefits and back into independent living.

We also have the support of W Bro Paul Henry who owns Wardle & Keech in Northampton and Proctors in Cambridge and he has moved free of charge, 106 victims of domestic abuse.

Bro Matt Horton, who owns Home Outlets, has provided beds, wardrobes, coffee tables and sofas and any furniture we need when we house homeless friends free of charge.

This whole operation is funded by the 3 Pillars-Feeding the Homeless and Supporting the Community.

We have another new venture, with our close friends, "Caring for Cambridgeshire Homeless".

There are two Founder members, Karen Keech and Karen Gibbs, who started this just over 6 years ago. Karen Keech and her team take food and toiletries round the streets of Cambridge with their trolleys, visiting all the homeless at their particular pitches.

We now join her once fortnightly with our charity van, park up near the Market Square, and serve hot food and drinks from the Van as well as providing sleeping bags, clothes etc. We are currently receiving 20-25 visitors, including women, who are sleeping on the streets.

Karen is like a guardian angel to these people and has a wonderful support team of lead volunteers, ably supported by hubby Lawrence, when he is available.

  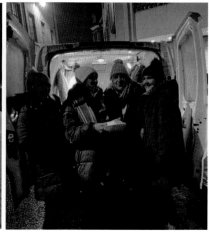

We have always helped each other and will continue to do so.

ST NEOTS FACEBOOK POLL:

A poll was conducted to find the most popular charity or business in St Neots & District.

There were over 1400 entrants.

The 3 Pillars Feeding the Homeless won the poll with well over 1000 votes and over 30% of the votes.

Wood Green Animal Shelter came second with just under 100 votes less.

NOVEMBER 2021- PRESENTATION OF MAYORS CHARITY FUND.

Former Mayor, Stephen Ferguson, presented 3 Pillars with a cheque & said that The 3 Pillars were the finest charity he had ever witnessed in St Neots - PRAISE INDEED!

The Town Council also awarded us a grant of £10,000.00 towards the cost of our new unit at The Mortgage Brokers premises.

<u>We cannot thank enough all the councillors that granted us this money.</u>

THANKYOU LETTER FROM LOCAL MP JONATHAN DJANOGLY:

THOMAS MORRIS ESTATE AGENTS- SIMON BRADBURY:

"Firstly, I've got to say what a totally incredible organisation Three Pillars really is. The fact that it offers REAL practical help to those in need locally is so impressive. To be honest, until I came across Three Pillars about 5 years ago I wasn't even aware of the issue of homelessness in and around our own community – I thought it was something that was an issue " somewhere else "… how wrong I was!

In those 5 years or so, we at Thomas Morris have been very proud to be associated with this inspiring charity and to help out with more than just much needed funds. We've provided a number of colleagues to help with distribution of food to the homeless in Peterborough, provided food items for those trips and assisted with food parcels delivered to the people of St.Neots which fits in very well with our foodbank campaigns and other activities that we do to support our marvellous community. In the last 6 months alone we have donated over £4,000 to Three Pillars which we have raised by various means including a " Sleepout " on the streets of St.Neots on one of the coldest nights of the year!

We've done this simply because they do so much good and offer much needed support to those in need."

Simon Bradbury - Managing Director of Thomas Morris

(Left to right: Myself, Richard Carpenter of Thomas Morris Estate Agents, Ged Dempsey)

KAREN KEECH- CO-FOUNDER OF "CARING FOR CAMBRIDGESHIRE HOMELESS" GROUP

"Great things can happen when inspired by Team Work! So when two likeminded, but very different groups join forces, wonderful things happen.

A few years ago I stumbled upon a group called 3 Pillars Feeding the Homeless when I read someone's post on Facebook asking for some donations of clothing for the homeless. Homelessness was something close to my heart and I myself had recently joined a group who supported people living on the streets in Cambridge. The group Caring for Cambridgeshire's Homeless (CCH) was formed shortly after I joined.

I remember back in the early days when everything at 3 Pillars was stored on a double decker bus and I would often come to the bus to bring donations or ask Mick if I could search for a pair of trainers or a coat for someone in need if I didn't have the required item in my own stock. Everyone at 3 Pillars was so kind and accommodating and never minded me turning up to raid their supplies.

I have very fond memories of volunteering at the Brewery Tap in Peterborough with Mick, Vernon and Ged and the wonderful team of people who handed out a hearty meal and supplies to the people waiting eagerly for the van to arrive. On the occasions I helped, I was given a great insight into how 3 Ps worked in contrast to how we conducted our voluntary outreaches with CCH.

My group set about walking around the streets of Cambridge with trolleys loaded full of supplies, whereas Mick and his team had a great spread set out on trestle tables with a queue of hungry customers patiently waiting in line to eat their hot dinner. These outreaches were not only a chance for people to stock up on desperately needed provisions and eat a hot meal, but a chance to talk and be heard, to have some social interaction and for a couple of hours, to not feel invisible. The evenings were full of kindness, care and compassion highlighted by the incredible work carried out by 3 Pillars.

Over the years it has been an absolute privilege to work alongside Mick Pescod and his team of devoted volunteers. Nothing is ever too much trouble for them and Ged has always been on hand if we have needed support with a particular concern.

During the Covid years the work carried out by both groups had to be modified with 3 Pillars doing great things to support our local community and of course our own outreaches at CCH changed dramatically. We had to cease our monthly hot food events and we were pretty devastated that we were no longer able to get the hot dinners out to those in need. But guidelines had to be followed.

So when Mick approached me with the idea of joining forces to enable us to get those hot meals and supplies back to the homeless and vulnerably housed I jumped at the chance. From the start, our collaborative outreaches proved a great hit with volunteers from both groups joining forces to get the job done.

Mick and his team have become regular visitors to the streets of Cambridge and the street folk look forward to visiting the van for a hearty hot dinner, a chance to stock up on supplies or quite simply come for a chat and a chance to offload their worries to a group of compassionate volunteers ready to offer an all-important listening ear and a shoulder to cry on.

I think it's safe to say the volunteers at 3 Pillars gained an insight into life living in a shop doorway and I'll never forget the expression on Mick's face when he saw the cardboard home of an elderly lady which she'd set up in a door way. Cardboard walls adorned the shop front to protect her from the elements as well as the unwanted stares of passers-by. Mick's expression was one of bewilderment.

Many people arrive at the van to stock up on clothes then immediately head for the nearby public toilets where they wash with the wipes we supply and change into the new clothes we give them. We see the effects on people who have no place to call home, how they eat their dinner like they've not had a hot meal in days and thank us profusely for treating them like humans. It's humbling to say the least.

It means everything to the volunteers at Caring for Cambridgeshire's Homeless to have Mick and the team supporting us in such a significant way, but not as much as it does to the street folk of Cambridge whose eyes light up at the sight of the van as it approaches our usual spot.

It's onwards and upwards for the two groups as we have increased the outreaches to weekly visits, bringing some warmth, comfort and kindness to those in desperate need."

A rare social evening together courtesy of the Nawab restaurant.

A REALITY OF CHARITY

Both of our large vans have been vandalised on separate occasions & were off the road for several months each time. Despite CCTV & secure parking, the vandals dismantled the vans & were never apprehended. This was a setback but as usual we all rallied together to ensure that our street friends didn't miss out on a hot meal & the elderly & vulnerable got their fresh food deliveries as usual. We are now back to normal working thanks to Aaron & his team at A.G. Motors who fixed the second van free of charge!

<u>Summary of the last 8 years</u>

We have helped arrange accommodation for 116 homeless and numbers keeps increasing. All donated by our supporters, we have given out to the homeless, needy and vulnerable people about 60,000 fresh food bags, plus grocery bags, enormous quantities of tents, sleeping bags, clothing, trainers, joggers, jeans, boxers, shirts, hoodies, coats, ladies clothing, toiletries………. and a never ending supply of chats, warm smiles & laughter!

We now also have our very own fantastic pin badge designed by my granddaughter Scarlet & kindly manufactured, marketed & distributed by Martin & Kindred Faulks of Lewis Masonic.

All profits are going to help our street friends. If you would like to purchase one please go to https://www.lewismasonic.co.uk/three-pillars-feeding-the-homeless-pin-badge.htm

Thank you to everyone for making a difference!
Mick

Final Note: Due to health issues over the last 18 months, I announced my retirement in November 2023 & I would just like to thank all those who sent me messages appreciation, which I will treasure forever.

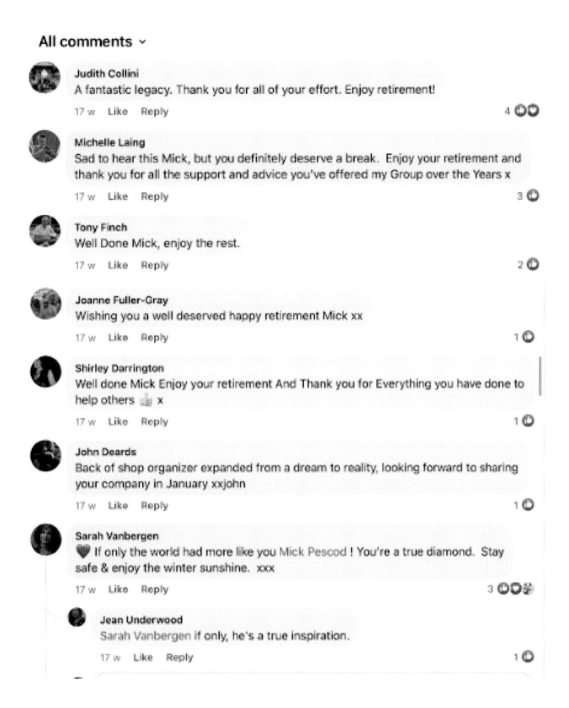

All comments ⌄

Judith Collini
A fantastic legacy. Thank you for all of your effort. Enjoy retirement!
17 w   Like   Reply   4

Michelle Laing
Sad to hear this Mick, but you definitely deserve a break. Enjoy your retirement and thank you for all the support and advice you've offered my Group over the Years x
17 w   Like   Reply   3

Tony Finch
Well Done Mick, enjoy the rest.
17 w   Like   Reply   2

Joanne Fuller-Gray
Wishing you a well deserved happy retirement Mick xx
17 w   Like   Reply   1

Shirley Darrington
Well done Mick Enjoy your retirement And Thank you for Everything you have done to help others 👍 x
17 w   Like   Reply   1

John Deards
Back of shop organizer expanded from a dream to reality, looking forward to sharing your company in January xxjohn
17 w   Like   Reply   1

Sarah Vanbergen
🤍 If only the world had more like you Mick Pescod ! You're a true diamond. Stay safe & enjoy the winter sunshine. xxx
17 w   Like   Reply   3

   Jean Underwood
   Sarah Vanbergen if only, he's a true inspiration.
   17 w   Like   Reply   1

Markie Reeds
A simple act turned into a big vision. All the best, you've earned a big rest.

17 w   Like   Reply   2 👍

Christine Campen
Good luck in the future You truly are inspirational and so many owe their life to you
Thank you 🖤🖤

17 w   Like   Reply   2 👍🤗

Rebecca Wells
Wishing you a wonderful Retirement 🖤 thank you for being one of God's angels on
Earth to help others 🙏

17 w   Like   Reply   1 👍

Daniel Cooke
Mick Pescod you have achieved something amazing Mick, enjoy your retirement and
thank you for everything you've done

17 w   Like   Reply   2 👍🤗

Yvette Hadley
You will be missed greatly, 🙏 🖤

17 w   Like   Reply   2 👍❤️

Julia Sinclair-Brown
Enjoy your well-deserved retirement. You're a true inspiration 🖤

17 w   Like   Reply   2 👍

Mick Vernalls
Well done Mick enjoy your retirement well deserved 👏🍺

17 w   Like   Reply   1 👍

Luke Wooding
You are an inspiration and truly remarkable guy Mick Pescod congratulations on all
that you achieved with the 3 Pillars. Such a fantastic job. Now go and enjoy
retirement in the sunshine

17 w   Like   Reply   7 👍❤️🤗

Jean Smith
Hope you enjoy your retirement Mick you certainly deserve it. Hope the scans show
good results.   Best wishes to you and your wife, hope winter break does you good.
👍

17 w   Like   Reply   1 👍

Donna Wooding
Wishing you all the best Mick in your well deserved retirement xx

17 w   Like   Reply   1 👍

Helen Bright
God bless you Enjoy your well deserved retirement. Hope your scan shows
something easily remedied xxx

17 w   Like   Reply   1 👍

Gemma Hull

Aww this is sad to read and very heart felt. You are one of the kindness men I have ever met. You helping me by allowing me to join in and help others really saved me in the toughest times in my life. The works needs more men like you Mick Pescod xxx

17 w   Like   Reply   3 👍❤️

Diane Monahan

Wow! You certainly deserve to retire! You have made so much difference to so many people! Enjoy your well earned rest! xx

17 w   Like   Reply   1 ❤️

Helen Distill-Elder

Going to be missed Mick Pescod take care and enjoy x

17 w   Like   Reply   1 ❤️

Pip Lee

You are a very special man & have created a very special legacy! Enjoy your retirement xxx

17 w   Like   Reply   3 ❤️

Shelley Cox

All the best

17 w   Like   Reply   1 ❤️

Alison Clarke

Wishing you good health and a long and happy retirement Mick 😊

Fiona Ledsham

Your an amazing man who has helped so many people, enjoy your retirement, you truly deserve it xx

17 w   Like   Reply   1 ❤️

Nicola Speed

Thank you Mick for caring and going over and above to help those in need, such a great role model, I wish you a well deserved rest.

17 w   Like   Reply   1 ❤️

Paula Stanford

You so deserve your retirement Mick, you've worked hard and got things done for so so many people. 🖐️ I first met you over 30 years ago when you became my insurance man and obviously the football with Ian, so you've always been on the go lol. Enjoy your well earned rest, hope your health improves and enjoy your holiday with Lorain. Thank you

17 w   Like   Reply   1 ❤️

Maureen Childerley

Well done you have done very good job best wishes Mick for your retirement

17 w   Like   Reply   1 ❤️

Yvonne Bailey

Enjoy your retirement, what a wonderful legacy to leave, you must feel proud! X

17 w   Like   Reply   1 ❤️

Meenakshi Sharma

Gerard Thomas Dempsey am sure it will but it won't be the same without Mick Pescod.. he is the heart & soul of this charity.. the human touch , deep care, and the selflessness is not everyone's forte.... I am so sad reading this but will carry on , only to keep Micks legacy going . Thankyou Mick for this gift of humanity you have given 🙏🖤🙏

17 w   Like   Reply   4 👍👍

Gerard Thomas Dempsey

Meenakshi, Mick made a major contribution to the Charity and it will always be remembered and recognised.

We will continue to support all the locations we have established and expand our support to the most vulnerable in our community.

We are grateful for all the support you give and do pleased you are going to continue.

17 w   Like   Reply   1 👍

Emily Jane

everyone who works for this wonderful charity is selfless , or we wouldn't be volunteers. Everyone has done their own part to build this amazing team. Well done Ged and Mick for creating such a wonderful charity, and good luck to mick in his retirement 🙏😊

17 w   Like   Reply   2 👍👍

Susie Watts

Thank you for your kindness 🖤

17 w   Like   Reply   1 👍

Joanne Johnson

Good luck with your scan next week. Thank you for helping so many people. X

17 w   Like   Reply   1 👍

Angie Collins

What a legacy... we have all done the little bits but having such an impact - and an ongoing one is incredibly special... wishing you improved and hopefully good health in your retirement.
Job well done 🖤

17 w   Like   Reply   1 👍

Gerard Thomas Dempsey

Mick, we will carry on and your contribution has been immense. The Charity will continue with its work and the plans are to extend the service to Corby, Kettering and Wellingborough in the New Year.

Since we started 8 years ago we have facilitated housing for 198 street friends of which 89 of those are working off benefits and back into independent living.

We now feed 85+ in Peterborough, 90+ in Northampton and 15+ in Rushden. We provide tents, sleeping bags, clothes and toiletries at these sites and support fixed sites in Peterborough.

Rules

Andrew Turner

thanks mick you will be missed by us all especially jazz

17 w   Like   Reply   1 👍

Robert Donaldson
All the very best Mick Pescodd go and enjoy yourself brother..kick back and have some you time

17 w   Like   Reply   1 👍

Kayleigh Shaw
Absolutely incredible!

17 w   Like   Reply   1 👍

Denise Hillier
Enjoy your retirement, you have served the homeless people well. Now it's time to look after yourself, health comes first, the younger ones can continue what you brought to fruition. Don't know you personally, I'm a volunteer at St. James Three Pillars so follow all what's going on. Good luck Mick x

17 w   Like   Reply   3 👍

Karen Keech
Still can't believe it!
Not sure what we'll do without you Mick!
A true gentleman! The kindest man with the biggest heart always there to listen and lend a helping hand.
Your support has been immense.
Thank you for everything 🖤
PS you're not getting rid of me that easily ... I'll see you on FaceTime 😊

17 w   Like   Reply   6 👍👍

> **Michaela J Couzens**
> Karen Keech Im right with you there Karen xxxxxxx
>
> 17 w   Like   Reply   2 👍👍

Doug Terry
You and your team have done an amazing job over the Mick.
Some how I think after a nice winter break you will be back.
You wouldn't know what to do with your spare time and the misses will complain about getting under feet..

17 w   Like   Reply   1 👍

Lorraine Burdett
Well done for all your hard work. Time to look after yourself. Enjoy your retirement. 🖤👏👏👏👏

17 w   Like   Reply   2 👍

Emily Jane
Enjoy your retirement mick, all the best x

17 w   Like   Reply   2 👍

Mark Colmer
Wishing you all the best Mick, enjoy your retirement. You will be greatly missed

17 w   Like   Reply   1 👍

Simone Warren
Mick you are one of the rarest diamonds in this often-too-heartless world. On behalf of the whole community, I want to say a big thank you from the bottom of all our hearts 💚💚💚 x

17 w   Like   Reply   2 👍

Clare Szczepanski
You really are an inspirational man Mick. You have set up an amazing organisation, and helped so many, your dedication over the years to help those in need has been outstanding.
Wishing you better health and enjoy a well deserved retirement 🖤 x

17 w   Like   Reply   1

Tony Greene
Thanks for all you have done Mike many the foundations laid by you continue on 👏 👏👏👏

17 w   Like   Reply   1

Jo Snooks
Wishing you a happy well earned retirement Mick. You should be very proud of what you have started x

17 w   Like   Reply   1

Hazel Thomson
Thank you Mick for everything from the beginning and now, I wish you well with your health and have a very happy retirement which is well deserved.

17 w   Like   Reply   1

Sue Peacock
What you've achieved has been amazing!! Enjoy your retirement, you've certainly earned it. 👏 👏👏🖤

17 w   Like   Reply   1

Ivana Baldissera
Enjoy your retirement you have earned it plus more and thank you for all you've done for our street friends 👏👏🙏

17 w   Like   Reply   1

Chriss Camp
Best wishes on your retirement Mick Pescod and congratulations on everything you have achieved with 3 pillars 👏

17 w   Like   Reply   1

Chris McCabe
All the best for a peaceful retirement.

17 w   Like   Reply   1

Toni Bourne
You are a true diamond, Mick, and will be so missed xx 🕊

17 w   Like   Reply   1

Linda Tongue
Good 🍀 luck with your onward journey

17 w   Like   Reply

Christine Anne
Happy retirement Mick! May you stay in good health and enjoy it x

17 w   Like   Reply

Lois Ashton Bowey
What an inspiration you are Mick... never have I ever met such a lovely man. You helped me so so much when I moved here. Gave me help, support, confidence, and made me where I am today, thank you. You will be missed by everyone. I hope your scan results come out all okay. Enjoy your retirement, you deserve it. Hope to stay in contact with you still.. lots of love mick xxxx

17 w   Like   Reply   3

Mary D'Cruz
My Son Desmond and I wish you a Happy and restful retirement. You have earned it. Thank You for all the hard work you did for the The Three Pillars feeding the Homeless. You will be missed. Wishing you well soon. We hope you and your wife Lorain have a wonderful holiday.

17 w   Like   Reply   1 ⬤

Zoe Masterson
What a legacy you have left and it shows the power of "Acts of kindness". Lives have changed because of you! Enjoy your retirement and thank you x

17 w   Like   Reply   2 ⬤

Anne Murgatroyd
Wishing you all the best and happy holiday and hope you enjoy your self xx

17 w   Like   Reply   1 ⬤

Terry Cadby
Well done Mick best wishes to you mate 👍

Maureen Collins
Good luck for the future Mick,
You really are an inspirational man. Enjoy your retirement x

17 w   Like   Reply   1 ⬤

Caroline Chattwell Grint
Enjoy your retirement Mick what a legacy to leave behind. A well deserved break after all the good you and the team have done xxx

17 w   Like   Reply   2 ⬤

Nikki Linford
What you have done has been amazing . Enjoy your retirement x

17 w   Like   Reply   1 ⬤

Emma Gough
Well done. The world would be a better place with more people like you in it.

17 w   Like   Reply   1 ⬤

Alex Thomson
Mick Pescod. You have achieved an unbelievable amount and helped countless people. Enjoy your retirement. You are the epitome of a good human being 🙏

17 w   Like   Reply   2

Andy Henry
Mick your efforts will be continued by the team and those who are helped in the future will be by an amazing team who stand on your shoulders.

Candy Saunders
Enjoy your retirement, you have certainly earned it and should be extremely proud of all that you achieved and all that you have helped.Well done

17 w   Like   Reply   1 👍

Ian Robertson
Have a great break mick, enjoy...
And enjoy your retirement, a fantastic achievement well done mate x

17 w   Like   Reply   1 👍

Simon Sherratt
Mick, your legacy is immense, your thoughtfulness knows no bounds and your retirement is so thoroughly deserved. Enjoy every moment 👏👏👏xx

17 w   Like   Reply   1 ❤️

Kim Rossiter
You're an inspiration, enjoy your retirement

17 w   Like   Reply

Jules Sismey
An amazing chap thanks xxx

17 w   Like   Reply

Sandra Cullis
Go off and enjoy your retirement Mick, you need to take care of yourself. You have done a marvellous job starting the wonderful organisation and you should be proud 👏. I'm sure the good work will continue through the brilliant hard working team behind the scenes, you all do a great job thank you you all.

17 w   Like   Reply   1 👍

Bex Johnson
I can't even remember what year I joined as a volunteer, albeit not an active one anymore due to my own health/work issues but has always been a pleasure to work alongside you

17 w   Like   Reply   1 👍

Jan Dorman
You will be sorely missed. Thank you. X

17 w   Like   Reply   1 👍

David Jackman
Well done Mick, you are an unbelievable person and you have done so much to help others and put others first, all the very best in your retirement, look after yourself and hope all goes well with the MRA scan, all the very best Mick. 👍

17 w   Like   Reply   1 👍

Nicky Warnock
Thank you for everything you've done to make people's lives better Mick. Enjoy your well deserved retirement xxx

Rick Holden

All the best Mick Pescod, an absolute legend x

17 w   Like   Reply   1

Vernon Paine

Sad days but what a legacy left. He is Mr 3Ps

You all are so aware how much he does for people at a drop of a hat but few know how much he has done for me, he was there at the right time in the right place, if it wasn't for him who knows where I would be........ 6 years on he's been best man at my wedding we go on holidays together we play golf together and I am part of his family as he is mine we will always keep that bond (silly old fooker) but he will be sadly missed by the people in need but I know he will still be watching and helping and teaching me new skills...... love ya xxx

17 w   Like   Reply   9

Jackie Fitzpatrick

True inspiration and what a legacy to leave - thank you 🙏 😊 take care you of and yr family now 💜 absolute legend xx

17 w   Like   Reply   1

Emma Lambert

Wow mick what an amazing back story!! 🐢 enjoy your retirement and I'm sure those thousands of people wish you the same xxx

17 w   Like   Reply   1

Ann Walsh

What an inspiration you are Mick . You so deserve to retire and slow down. I hope the MRI scan goes well and they can sort your dizziness and tinnitus. Enjoy your holiday and have a lovely Christmas.

Congratulations on your retirement and thank you for making a big difference to our homeless friends. 👏👏👏👏👏👏 xx

17 w   Like   Reply   2

Abby Red

Amazing thing to do! Enjoy a rest xx

17 w   Like   Reply   1

Anne Grove

Enjoy your retirement, sounds like you have earned it 👍 Best wishes and all the best from my hubby, Johnny Grove, from football a good few years ago👏👍

17 w   Like   Reply   1

Wendy Bleech
Bless you Mick you are an angel. Look after yourself hey x

17 w   Like   Reply   1 👍

Ali Pearce
Aw Mick you are a fabulous kind hearted man and we will still see you around as always [?] what a fantastic start to the 3 pillars you have done xxx 😄

17 w   Like   Reply   1 👍

Lisa Bouland
God bless you 💜

17 w   Like   Reply   1 👍

David Shortall
You're an absolute inspiration Mick. A socialist in the purest sense of the word. Thank you so much for making a difference.

17 w   Like   Reply   3 😍👍

Anne Southwood
Wishing you a happy & healthy retirement Mick Pescod. Amazing work you have done. 😊

17 w   Like   Reply   1 👍

Ashley Ground
God bless you Mick, thank you for everything you've done.

Helen Beaumont
It's been a real pleasure to work alongside you these past few years and I know I speak for a lot of people when I say you will be missed!
Just make sure to still pop to the unit with Dottie occasionally! xxx

17 w   Like   Reply   4 👍

Charlotte Simpson
Thank you so so much for everything you have done. You have worked tirelessly to create and sustain a much needed and greatly appreciated service. With such strong foundations; its legacy will long continue whilst you enjoy your well deserved retirement. X

17 w   Like   Reply   1 👍

Michele Utting
What an amazing story. You are an inspiration. Enjoy your retirement 👏

17 w   Like   Reply   1 👍

Alan Barnett
Enjoy your retirement Mick, you certainly deserve it, 😊

17 w   Like   Reply   1 👍

Denise Cathrall

Happy Retirement Mick, you're a unique miracle at the heart of our community & what a legacy to leave, well done & thank you for making a difference when people really need it. Barry & I enjoyed coffee with you today xx

17 w   Like   Reply   1 😊

Tracey Usher

Aw Mick that retirement is so well deserved! You have done the most wonderful thing and helped so many people!

I hope your tests go well! Hats off to you and your amazing team xx

17 w   Like   Reply   1 😊

Sheridan Howcroft

Sending lots of love to you. Enjoy your retirement again

17 w   Like   Reply   1 😊

Michelle Kelly

Fantastic x

17 w   Like   Reply   1 😊

Jason Anderson

Fantastic work and you have left a great legacy, feet up now 👍 🙌

17 w   Like   Reply   1 😊

Kerry Walsh

We all absolutely adore you Mick Pescod. I can only echo what others have said. You are amazing. Thank you for everything you do.
You always find a way you can do something difficult and that is why 3 Pillars is where it is now. You didn't give up!
We will miss you so much. 🖤

17 w   Like   Reply   4 😊😊

Lynne Carol

Sp proud of what you have build up x long may it continue xxx

17 w   Like   Reply   1 😊

Lora Rance

Well done. X

17 w   Like   Reply   1 😊

Sheila Brighton

Bless you and have long and happy retirement !!

Melanie Greenhead
You're an absolute credit to our town. So proud of The 3 Pillars. Enjoy your retirement x

17 w   Like   Reply   1

Mike Abbott
Thank you for your service and generosity Mick Pescod, enjoy 'retirement'

17 w   Like   Reply   1

Clare Henry Was Tyler
What an amazing job you have done! Enjoy your well deserved rest xx

17 w   Like   Reply   1

Matthew Fox
Happy retirement

17 w   Like   Reply   1

Steve Williams
Mick Pescod - you're a legend bro. Proud to call you a brother.

Never forget, whatever you do should be without detriment to yourself - you have given freely, now its time to step back and look at the foundations you have laid with great pride.

Thanks to your wisdom and strength, the beauty of the 3 Pillars will continue to help those most in need 🙏 😎

Liz Nolan
Enjoy your retirement Mick, I remember that day in Oxford Street and was in awe of your thoughtfulness and kindness and how is went on to be a massive legacy to you. Well done have a wonderful retirement, you have been amazing 👏

17 w   Like   Reply   1

> **Mick Pescod**
> Liz Nolan
> That was some weekend Liz, it certainly changed my life.
>
> 17 w   Like   Reply

> Write a reply...

Karen Staines
Happy retirement Mick. You have been brilliant helping the homeless people.

17 w   Like   Reply   1

Peter Ellis
Mick,Thank you for your dedication.All the best in "retirement"

17 w   Like   Reply   1

Kim Oliver
A well deserved retirement Mick. You have done an amazing job that has inspired other people to do the same. What a wonderful legacy helping the most vulnerable xxx

17 w   Like   Reply   1

Lauren Wilding
What a wonderful achievement you have created! Enjoy your retirement xx

17 w   Like   Reply   1

Vicky Borman
🖤🖤🖤🖤

17 w   Like   Reply   1

Ann Hollowell
I congratulate you Mike / so many people have and will continue to benefit and be comforted by your courageous venture.
I wish you good health and happiness for the future .

17 w   Like   Reply   1

Peter Coulston
Well done Mick, so many people over the years have benefited from your efforts and dedication. Enjoy yourself winding down, keep safe and healthy. I'll carry on supplying my yearly package. All the best.

16 w   Like   Reply   1

Shirley Harradine
Thank you for all you have done for the people who have nothing . Enjoy your retirement & I wish you good health.

16 w   Like   Reply   1

Conner Hodge
Inspiration to us all

16 w   Like   Reply   1

Sarah Green
What an incredible human being you are Mick. I hope you enjoy your retirement

16 w   Like   Reply   1

Jayne Miller
What great things you achieved in that time Mick you have worked miracles to help the homeless. You deserve your retirement and I hope it's a long and happy one !!! I really hope your health improves to . You have made a big difference to many lives
👏👏👏👏

16 w   Like   Reply   1

Caroline Deeprose
You leave an incredible legacy behind you. All the best xxx

16 w   Like   Reply   1

51

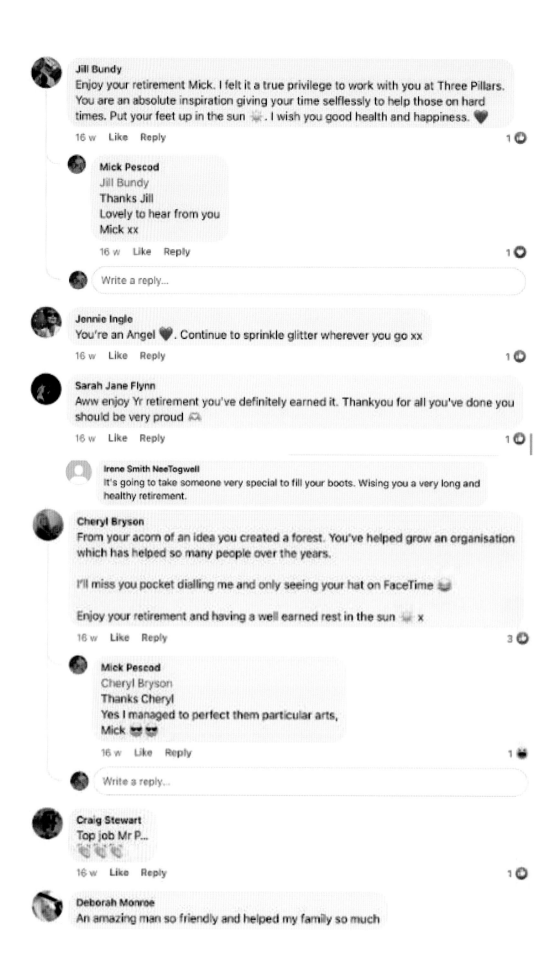

Jill Bundy

Enjoy your retirement Mick. I felt it a true privilege to work with you at Three Pillars. You are an absolute inspiration giving your time selflessly to help those on hard times. Put your feet up in the sun 🌞. I wish you good health and happiness. 🖤

16 w   Like   Reply   1 ♡

> **Mick Pescod**
> Jill Bundy
> Thanks Jill
> Lovely to hear from you
> Mick xx
>
> 16 w   Like   Reply   1 ♡
>
> Write a reply...

Jennie Ingle

You're an Angel 🖤. Continue to sprinkle glitter wherever you go xx

16 w   Like   Reply   1 ♡

Sarah Jane Flynn

Aww enjoy Yr retirement you've definitely earned it. Thankyou for all you've done you should be very proud 🤗

16 w   Like   Reply   1 ♡

> **Irene Smith NeeTogwell**
> It's going to take someone very special to fill your boots. Wising you a very long and healthy retirement.

Cheryl Bryson

From your acorn of an idea you created a forest. You've helped grow an organisation which has helped so many people over the years.

I'll miss you pocket dialling me and only seeing your hat on FaceTime 😄

Enjoy your retirement and having a well earned rest in the sun 🌞 x

16 w   Like   Reply   3 ♡

> **Mick Pescod**
> Cheryl Bryson
> Thanks Cheryl
> Yes I managed to perfect them particular arts,
> Mick 😎😎
>
> 16 w   Like   Reply   1 👍
>
> Write a reply...

Craig Stewart

Top job Mr P...
👏👏👏

16 w   Like   Reply   1 ♡

Deborah Monroe

An amazing man so friendly and helped my family so much

Sandra Carey
Enjoy your very well earned rest Mick , your an absolute angel 🖤

17 w   Like   Reply   2 👍

Kevin Paul Morris
Mick you are a legend no words can describe the good you and the team do , to help the homeless is well appreciated and much needed

All the best

17 w   Like   Reply   3 👍👍

Alan Dodson
A wonderful legacy Mick , well done 👍

17 w   Like   Reply   2 👍

David Docherty
Absolutely fantastic Mick, enjoy your retirement you have earned it.

17 w   Like   Reply   1 👍

Jan Payne
Wishing you a happy and healthy retirement Mick.

17 w   Like   Reply   2 👍

Richard Harradine
Well done mate, it's so good to see and read all the good work that you and the team do. Happy retirement, enjoy the warmer climate....

Markie Reeds
A simple act turned into a big vision. All the best, you've earned a big rest.

17 w   Like   Reply   2 👍

Christine Campen
Good luck in the future You truly are inspirational and so many owe their life to you Thank you 🖤🖤

17 w   Like   Reply   2 👍😢

Rebecca Wells
Wishing you a wonderful Retirement 🖤 thank you for being one of God's angels on Earth to help others 🙏

17 w   Like   Reply   1 👍

Daniel Cooke
Mick Pescod you have achieved something amazing Mick, enjoy your retirement and thank you for everything you've done

17 w   Like   Reply   2 👍😢

Yvette Hadley
You will be missed greatly, 🙏🖤

17 w   Like   Reply   2 👍👍

Julia Sinclair-Brown
Enjoy your well-deserved retirement. You're a true inspiration 🖤

17 w   Like   Reply   2 👍

Special thanks to:

FOOD:

- Aldis Eaton Socon
- Christine Fairholm and Select Now
- Greggs Bakeries St Neots, Eaton Socon
- Hilary Grant
- Hotel Chocolat, Eaton Socon Warehouse
- Marie Town
- Meena Sharma
- Mel Ford,
- Sarah and Jenny Lewis
- Sarah Flack and Sawtry 3rd Year
- Tesco Eaton Socon

SPONSORS:

- Darren Pescod
- 4 Counties Lodge
- Ailwyn Lodge
- Black Cat Radio
- Chris Armiger- EXSC
- Country Fayre
- Fitzwilliam Lodge
- Glittering Star Lodge 322 (Irish Constitution)
- Granit Parts LP
- Gresham Lodge
- Hotel Chocolat
- Lams Rushden
- Lodge of Fidelity
- Masonic Bowls
- MCF
- Michael & Angela Kenyon
- Norse Lodge
- Northant & Hunts Mark Benevolent Association
- OSM St Lawrence's Conclave
- Premier Plus
- Provincial Grand Charity
- RAFA Club
- Richard & Sarah Vanbergen
- Richmond Hill Financial Limited
- Royal Order of Scotland
- St Ivo Lodge
- St Neots Golf Club
- St Neots Storage
- St Neots Town Council
- St Peter's Lodge
- TD Autos
- Thomas Morris

VOLUNTEERS PRESENT AND PAST:

- WB Aaron Day
- WB Adam Hillis (RIP)
- Abby Nortfield
- Ali & Don Pearce
- Amy Byfield
- Ann Walsh
- Barry & Denise Cathrall
- Barry Hayden
- WB Brian & Ann Downs
- Bridget Peeroo
- Bro Chris Eddy
- Bro John & Kath Lumley
- Bro Lee and April Garner
- Bro Rod Bissett
- Bro Roland Brown
- WB Cearse Marinaro
- Cheryl Bryson
- Clare Szczepanski
- Darren & Lita Pescod
- Don & Anne Murgatroyd
- Donna Wooding
- Emma Georgiou Fletcher
- Gemma Hull
- George - Rushden
- Gill Robb
- Hazel Goudie
- Heidi Cutter
- Helen Beaumont
- Helen Distill Elder
- Helen Gellatly
- Jade Horton
- Jenny Pinnock
- Jenny Johnson
- Jill Bundy
- Jill Jones
- Jo Burns
- John & Tracy Darlow
- Jo Whittaker
- WB John Rivett
- WB Justin Beaumount
- Jyoti Patel
- Karen Keech
- Karen Margie
- Kaye Cousins
- Keith Gotch
- Kerry Walsh

- WB Leighton Mills
- Lisa Bache Haley
- Lois Bowey
- Lorain Pescod
- Maddy Ellis
- Marina Hollinghead
- Mark Adams
- Mark Colmer
- Mark Torode
- Mary D'Cruz
- Maureen Morris
- Meena Sharma
- Mike Kirby
- Natalie Glover
- Nicki Mulhausen
- Nigel & Jenny Ingle
- Paul and Sarah Pankhurst
- WB Paul Henry - Wardle & Keech
- Pip Lee
- Ray Cheryl
- Roland Brown
- WB Roy Sparks
- Roy Tucker
- Sandie Isaacs
- Scarlet Robinson
- Scott Owen
- Sheila Wren
- Shirley Darrington
- Simon & Carol John
- WB Simon Harper
- Steph Knowlton
- Street Vets
- Stuart Morgan
- Sue & Ivan Page
- Supported Housing Fellowship
- Susan Haresign
- Tara Ward
- Toni Bourne
- Vernon & Steph Paine
- Vicki Hill & Andy Hill
- Victoria Swallow & mum Jackie
- WB Vince Tindale
- WM Martin & Kitty Faulks

Sincere apologies to anyone whom I have missed out,
please put it down to senior moments. ☺